in praise of FOR LACK of DIAMOND YEARS

"FOR LACK of DIAMOND YEARS is pitch perfect, deeply felt yet not sentimental, an absolutely true-blue and richly unadorned dance with the language. Then there's the deft delineation of airy space within the poems—much like small songbirds hopping to flight after feeding. There isn't a dash here to be altered. A deep pleasure on the page."

– Holly Anderson

"These poems are extraordinary. Caroline Beasley-Baker's voice is unique, and strong, and like no other poet I know. She is the real deal, as they say—everything works, even the ravishingly brilliant ways that the poems appear on the page. For some reason, I keep thinking of Leonard Cohen's lines, 'There a crack in everything/That's how the light gets in.'"

– Richard Bruno

". . . vibrant, cut-shining poems . . ."

– Virginia McClure

"Caroline Beasley-Baker is her voice, working the faults and facets like a jeweler, but with language. She make parallels collide, no easy trick that."

– Bob Holman

D1405406

for
lack
of
diamond
years

Copyright © 2013 Caroline Beasley-Baker

This work is licensed under the Creative Commons Attribution-NonCommercial-NoDerivs 3.0 Unported License. To view a copy of this license, visit http://creativecommons.org/licenses/by-nc-nd/3.0/.

ISBN: 978-1-938349-09-6
Library of Congress Control Number: 2013933093

Grateful acknowledgment is made to the following publications, where some of these poems originally appeared—
La Fovea: "blush/in 3 colors," "calamity/calm in the cutaway in 5 colors," and "hesitate/the first blossom in 3 colors"; *Mobius, The Poetry Magazine*: "goodbye/going & gone?"; *The MOM Egg*: "fusion/star baby" and "headlong/all fall down"; *MungBeing Magazine*: "butterfly/undone," "carpenter/my captain & refrain," "dead/yet still our neurons fire back hello," "echo/boomerang or stick?", "faithful/by clock & compass," "helpmate/hold me back with love," "idyll/prince hal in 9 colors," "mythos/her limits are for her to know," "nativity/early spring," "NIGHTINGALE," "old-fashioned-robotic/a romance," "prairie/around the campfire," "preschool/eyes & ears," "rakshashi/into the unknown unknown," "red/lost & found," "repair/the prodigal self," "sea-shanty/iceland," "soothsay/mediterranea in 2 colors," "sun-up/sun-down (after rilke & thoreau)," "superstition/extremely longing," "trifle/isn't it romance?", "winter/now i lay me down in 3 colors," "wooing/one more frog goes a-courtin'"; *Qarrtsiluni*: "Our Rowdy Pack Song" (excerpt); *The Chained Hay(na)ku Project*, Meritage Press, 2010, San Francisco, CA: "Marine Acid Air" and "The OO OO Chain" (excerpts).

Design by C. Beasley-Baker
www.carolinebeasley-baker.com

Printed in the USA

First Pelekinesis Printing 2013
www.pelekinesis.com

Acknowledgments
My gratitude to poet/writer Holly Anderson for her thoughtful read of the final draft of this book—her passion for words, her generosity of spirit, inspire me to write as best I can. I am indebted to Mark Givens at Pelekinesis for his good critical judgment and kind support throughout bringing this book into the world. My appreciation is also due the Brevitas poets—especially Andrew Kaufman, Katrinka Moore, and Hal Sirowitz for their attention to the first versions of some of these poems. My special thanks to Leila, Gloria, and Yvain—who taught me poetry in first place. And, as always, thanks to my family and friends—each one of them—I feel blessed in their company.

for
lack
of
diamond
years

poems by

CAROLINE BEASLEY-BAKER

for my daughter ❖

This Jack, joke, poor potsherd, ' patch, matchwood, immortal diamond,
Is immortal diamond.

— GERARD MANLEY HOPKINS

❖ **preamble/beginnings**

he sits drinking beer in the center of the kitchen — a big man
on a too-small wooden chair. he rocks back on 2 legs of the chair
and they all laugh as the 2-year-old girl — loving the bittersweet
— climbs into his lap to claim him:

sing old shep.

they all hush for a moment before his fine tenor begins:

when i was a lad and old shep was a pup . . .

thumb in mouth/her ear to his heart — she rocks as she cries —
falling fast asleep to their laughter.

poems & mesostics

poems & mesostics

poems & mesostics

faithful/by clock & compass

each morning she and the spotted dog step from the porch
— walk-trotting east into the Sonoran desert.

she counts as she goes to mark time
until a sparrow hawk — for example — flies south

calling her to restart
the step-count and follow . . .

and so it goes until they find themselves
reoriented to west and home.

then one day — sun-blinded while pivoting west —
she steps off a cliff into opaque air and the dog leaps to
follow . . .

she thinks only this:

crazy dog — *the proof is in the pudding* —
at the very least you have always attended to your own
true north . . .

and now my love — we float we flow we fly?

yang/black hole among circle & flow

did you know
an enigmatic-maw
commandeers

this galaxy
from-dead-center —
renders the eddy

useless/upends
our gyrating
hearts — sending us

to harrow
an-untidy-row
through the stars?

merrily-merrily-merrily
— as we go?

seafarer/2 a.m. & wide awake

tie me upright to the mast
of the ghost ship *Benignity*
whose absent captain
and crew transport each of us —
tucked safely in our bunks
below deck —
through the [blank]
of raw unknowing.

tie me to the mast:
do you see the sheen of glitter
— this cresting/thoughtless sea?

sun-up/sun-down (after rilke & thoreau)

what/now?

the night falls
gently —
oh-so-gently —
on a good day's work

— & now
my love?
do you lead me
toward the garden —

give me
this compensating night?
do you hold me back
with love —

or-cast-me-deep
beyond-the-oh-so-watchful stars?

or-nothing-of-the-kind.
the wood thrush sings —
& i am young again.
your shadow shifts/elides/

skirts each reveal . . .
yet still — i see this-coruscating-light —
b. dylan sings:

ride me high — you ain't going nowhere.

❖ blind-from-birth/no crystal ball

when you give birth to a child
how can you know where
her feet may fall?

who could've guessed
i'd find myself dancing on a table
in Bucharest with a Georgian who
had only one-half a neat ear intact?

who knew i'd see the face of
. . . *God* —
think only to kiss the offered brow
— then laugh?

tell me — who can scry the where/why
that is the map to my after life?
not me — not then — not now.

❖ torpor/tie me up tie me down

what kind of linger
binds me to this chair —
what dumb muscle-weight
keeps me sitting/doing
        nothing?
. . . heat — ambition listing off axis
— no will to heft.
                adrift . . .
why does that bird still sing —
that fucking horn honk?
my spirit — does she revel
in her own cool
mist — her no-
thingness?

winter/now i lay me down in 3 colors

if devotion were a color
would it be a Saccharin Mist —
a Scorching Passion —
or just Sky Blue?

a silly notion.
for my part i suspect
the true-devoted is scoured
of all but emanation and reflection:
existing wholly uncircumscribed —
a vessel of relegated desire.

∴

devotion — however manifest —
Saccharine/Scorching/Sky Blue
— is simply the calculation of light
transiting ice crystals or something like:

color — a trick/the beauty of refraction?

ascent/call me up from the dead

who stood at the bottom
of the rude stoop — crying — *Catullus*
        Catullus
                come to me now — come?
can you find me Catullus?
can i find you?
but then where in the midst of the starling chatter
— the wah/wahing of the cop car — the rash
rush/rushing — can we expect to find someone
who knows
        something of the bold clatter
of black branches scratching at the cold sky?

Nothing

fr**I**ghtens

a **G**reat

Heart —

Terrifying

Innocence

— a**N**gels

dis**G**raced —

un**A**dorned

Love

requit**E**s.

godsend/while waiting for the next comet

not nominal, numinous be.
— ANONYMOUS

what must it be to tell a tale
without constraint of the expected —
without unrecognized so . . .
reigning habit?

?/
without conceit to take our fire —

to make ashes of those myriad-
ever-flames/those choric voices that . . .
for want of wood/coal —
for lack of diamond years

— tell slowly/un-fire-like
their susurrus tales
of nights with voices:
reveling —

a rabble of tongues/ears . . .
the fugal chatter of ice/rock —
the hiss of all that surrounds and inter-
penetrates?

?/
coruscations of/a shiver of light?

fusion/star baby

The universe started out young and blue.
—ANONYMOUS/ASTROPHYSICIST

she opens the door —
sunlight hitting her straight on.
her eyes ignite beyond blue —
and there he is — his face in shadow
— when a solitary spark combusts
between them:

not magic/not metaphor . . .
just the blue fact of it.

which celtic or hindu deities?
who can guess —
            galaxies collide —
stars carom/hurtle/twist/eclipse —

caesura . . . *all is grace and fever pitch.*

repair/the prodigal self

do you remember?
he's just left you — no last minute reprieve.
there you are in Sausalito —
in the middle of the restaurant parking lot —
sitting on your suitcase — crying:

a 20-year-old's respectable

sturm und drang . . .

what could he be thinking?

i reach through my memory and touch you —
blond girl in your short/short dress — those ex-
pensive shoes . . .
look at us now.

here we are —
busy codifying all of that heartbreak/joy —
skirting order and the drift of words.
i know you can see — his way-too-blue eyes/
that cleft chin can't disguise his feckless nature.

have you even one thing of worth in common?

you almost know you can't re-make his mind —
be gracious —
        his gut (if not his head) is clear:

return the ring/let him go . . .
wear that yellow dress you have tucked away.

old-fashioned-robotic/a romance

ro- ro- ro-
your bodacious
botica

all the way
down
the-slip-slip stream —

a-rev-rev-revelation
of tinsel stars/
of triple-wah-trombones.

ro- ro- ro-
your outrageous
botica

straight-back-where
All Pieces&Parts
come to-dance/to-play —

animate/
inanimate things
done-up in chrome

— spray-painted
neoprene — isinglass?
surprise-me-now in organza

my-Boadicea-tintype —
matériel mine —
why don't you

ro-ro-ro —
back my way
so-unabashedly robotica

— let's parlay.

❖ blush/in 3 colors

CAPUT?
my Mortem Fallow —
&-yet you/

you slowly
dress-me-my-love
— my Falu Red . . .

less/not one thing more

consider a featureless sky —
no clouds no color
no temperament or perspective.
imagine a modest word
zigzagging yin to yang —
the remorseless suzerain
a selfless rani. don't think
too much. a riddle a koan
a chimaera — a handful of stars
ceaselessly disrobing?

*a co***L***d*

*mo***O***n —*

*n***O**

*star***S**

*— fiv***E**

P*ale*

*jew***E***ls in*

*my h***A***nd —*

R*elics*

*—***L***ost*

*tear***S**.

nativity/early spring in 3 colors

heliotropic
hectare — punchdrunk
— i'm stunned in nascent

luxe:
ruched/dew-sugared
ground greening in-sync

— ur-pleasures
reified/demitassed
dark — replete.

deliver
me rinsed/
tricked out/clean —

Blueish
Gooseberry Blond
dyed Snow Pink.

❖ off-kilter/unstringing the stars

i'm-a-ring-'round-rosie-girl —
a hot-blue-star —
unhitched & free-wheeling:

synaptic trash —
caught sweet
in borrowed mercies

. . .

tilt/
tilt-a-whirl/twist —
we all fall-down . . .

i'm-one-of-seven-sisters —
a pleiade —
i-sashay into beatitude

— *do you unravel-like-me?*

hesitate/the first blossom in 3 colors

a-clutch-of-titmice re-
calibrate —
chide the unsprung
callery pear — not quite
clement

enough . . .
chilly. Dun-silver-y
out my window — me
hankering

after
the muddied threshold of some-house i've never

had
— its White-washed lintel ablaze
in early Citrine —
queen anne's
lace

claims the spot by the gate.

helpmate/hold me back with love

she loves him.

she's two and he's 40-something —
the second of her grandmother's four husbands.
he knows the moment he sees her —
she's for him:

she needs a dog/a turtle — why not a fish . . .
he sees her standing at the top of the basement stairs
of the beer joint where her aunt tends bar
— calling tenderly after the rats —

kittykittykitty . . .

& — on the off chance she might need him —
he moves in/steps up close —

come here little Chickadee — let's dance.

. . . what happened to him? did he remarry?

he's most likely dead now —
but she can't help but wonder — can he see her
— even at this distance — flirting/
smiling back?

carpenter/my captain & refrain

i sang the stars to impress you.
i captured all of your tears
and placed the sea just so —
at your feet. i made
the boat pulled-up beside you
with my own two hands.
let's sail away — *come-on/*
come on — let's sail away.

odalisque/mermaid as the sun sets in 3 colors

sugar
toes — cherries —
painted Ruby bright —

i'm
kaleidoscope bliss
in Cornflower bruises/

tattoos/
pearls — i'm
aurora briny glitter —

adamant and circumspect:

circumnavigation —
zero/naught — my
Dayglo Blush unfurls.

he **S**teals

Away

one n**I**ght

Leaving

y**O**u.

he fea**R**s

hi**S**

de**S**ire —

your f**A**ith

In

his **L**ove

— y**O**ur

Need.

commonsensical/love not war

when the mind turns petty —
the heart shrinks to the size of a dime
— the spirit —
      if we can find it —
loses luster/threatens to go dead —
then what's the choice?

. . . to continue to dwindle/to idle
in the muck — to be hateful?
or to allow sweetness —
      a mote/a grain of . . .
succor?

you choose — it may not be either/or
but instead some small in-between —
an idyll in the interstice of . . .
a love me/love me not?

❖ encounter/standing before a small giotto

what am i to think when a very-grown
and still-quite-handsome man
approaches me cold only to say —

you look like you do yoga/
you make me feel like i'm 8.

8? i'm drifting in the early 14th c. —
can't quite move my eyes away
from this muscled-jewel of a painting

. . . 8?
does he see in mid-sentence
my indifference to him isn't feigned —
does he mean he feels just-old-enough
            not to punch me?

or should i speak to him in Sanskrit —
then quick-duck?

homely/self-portrait with flowers

am sitting here with some 100 proof
singing along to Lucinda/*2 Kool 2 Be 4-Gotten* —
thinking my homebody geraniums are splendid
after their own fashion — bright and unaware
of just how many people find them *2 Kommon*
2 Be Konsidered.
but even from this distance across the room
i can feel the fuzz of their leaves —
the promise of sun —
the tidy sparrow.

❖ prairie/the reddest bird

can't catch me
a red-bird
a-shoo-fly

or snatch me
a gingham-bird —
don't-ask-why.

can't catch me
a falling-star
or-any-old-bird-will-do.

your
hair is
ash and honey —

my-skip-to-m'-lou —
please sing
to me forever . . .

any-old-song-will-do.

sea-shanty/iceland

the windows need cleaning —
let's polish off the year —
gather up all the leaves

— one x one —
we'll wash them/burnish them —
salute the dwindled sun.

we'll sing a parting song —
we'll take a boat across the spiked
& spiny sea —

before the true-frost —
before —
the whole-world turns cold.

headlong/all fall down

snow falling sometimes falls
like brief and winnowed
stars . . .

and stars fall like tears —

and whether we're blessed or not —
washed clean or not —
we fall too.

the angels — do they still fall?

if not from grace or God . . .
then unburdened
        by joy
                or grief —

do they simply fall?
falling — as we sometimes fall
— like tears?

the **S**un weeps
*i***N** hell
sub-zer**O** tears —
filigreed —**W**hite.

funk/in 6 colors

desperation
Fudge/Fuzzy-wuzz-ys
aren't enough cozy-or-sweet

to transfigure this Gainsboro-Damned-COLD

day.
no-no —
breathe — you say —
make Amethyst your mantra
— breathe

straight-through-Iris-into-a-translucent-moderate-
Violet . . .
say what? where've you gotten to while i'm trying
to sort

this absurdity?

mythos/her limits are for her to know

if i say — *look at me i touch the sky —*
                here and here . . .

you say — *no-no . . .*
only those with the precise downbeat
like me can leap to miraculous heights —
                do it this way
and perhaps with practice . . .

i don't skip a beat/waste my sky-breath
in reply — i think only to my sky-self — *no-no?*
                killjoy/inflated ass . . . are you blind?
& i go on about my sky-business

:

i live on sky — eat it as i please.
i touch the sky by the very soul of my sky-nature —
i do so/will continue to do so/have done so for
millennia — more!
is it arrogance after all to know the air i breathe —
the translucent blood that makes me tripartite:
me —
        i touch the sky — and me.

soothsay/mediterranea in 2 colors

cradle
me indiscreetly
in glory/mire —

in-thunder
i-swan dive
streaking echo bare —

a-Silver-
cipher-spark
levitates/falling down

— spins-out —
a-spinner stumbles
— obliterates the midday.

now-hush-hush —
i'm spin-drunk/
i'm glowing Gold.

echo/boomerang or stick?

when was the last time
i stood on the hill and shouted —
how long must i wait must i wait?
and loved in the stillness the listening
as the words ran so far away
it made me think — *come back come back*
— where are you off to in such a steady rush?
are you mischief   . . . a thief?
and where are you now i wonder —
are you one with a covey of words?
have you dropped out past time —
beyond retrieval?

superstition/extremely longing

after Ono No Kamachi/Japan/Heian Era

i
having no lock of his hair —
she wears her nightgown
inside out:

now — let me dream of him.

ii
lost in black-shell time
she sees from the inside out
where the stars are pale
and streaming —
the moon lies next to her —
stifled/white —
her heart turns inside out:

my love — i see only you.

butterfly/undone

slow —
caught beating-fast
against the waterfall

— so-riotous/
proud — my
startled heart's unstrung

— crushed —
exotica/delicious
glass — i tarantella

in stardusty-lanes
transfixed —
so daring surfeit:

bangles — antiphonal loud.

the **M**ultiplying
forg**E**tful
Dark
eras**E**d
your cl**A**im

on **M**e —
now a qui**E**t thrush
un**D**oes my
h**E**art — my
m**A**jesty.

❖ finery/unadorned

she
wants a nice
coat/a-few-jewels

— nothing
fancy/no-
thing too indiscreet —

a
few blood-dark
rubies edging her

lapels —
buttons bound
up in silk —

now and then —
a-shy-gardenia
in her-clean-hair.

clique/long to belong?

there're always lines —
waiting lists to get into clubs/groups
nobody with any sense should desire
to be a part of in the first place —

why is this?

. . . our insatiable yen to be preferred:
          please-choose-me-i'm-really-plum
— *now* — i'm-really-really-plum . . . ?

DNA — an indiscriminate yin/a collective yang . . . ?

yet it's possible to miss a cilia of this bio-goo —
when the special invitation comes —
my internal compass almost-always-spins
to a kind of lilting vague:

no/no thanks/i think not . . .

pre-school/the eyes & ears

i spent my first 4 years in a beer joint in downtown
Kansas City on the edge of hillbilly and honky tonk —
      the ever-praised hank williams . . .
but here's
    young ferlin husky/
        lefty frizzell/webb pierce —
shuffleboard pucks click-swatting the beat —
     beer glasses sliding the length of the bar
my aunt flo polishes when things are a bit slow.

there's talk about politics — *which do you like best*
sweet-pea — a Donkey/an elephant ? . . . the laughter —
my aunt lola sitting on my father's knee — my mother
leaping
     from off the top of the juke box:

ALL caught by the flash of uncle john's leica.
    & my grandmother liona . . . *well —*
as the genteel leila said:

that liona — she's a firecracker — you know —
she's half French/half Indian — fond of dancing & fishing
& . . .

well — never you mind — sit closer honey-dear —
i'll teach you a song.

whistling/tinker tailor

a noun a verb
an odd singularity
melodic counterpoint
to whatever bit of melancholy
or musing or whatever else
adorns the mood/the action
of a particular person only
in the absolute present. now
not so frequently heard
or musically accomplished —
a prodigal staccato
biding time?

 **red/lost & found**

the less love pities the beast, the more one sorrows.
— ANONYMOUS

heading out to grandma's house
under a poisoned moon —
a little red riding hood watches
as the streets fill with vampires
        and werewolves —

loveless/lovelorn — even the air
is cavernous   keen
for a quick caress —
a nip/suck/rip here and there.

much-too-tender to be tangled up
among the cruising-dead —
melancholy trumps fear
        as her fondest notions

disassemble . . .
virulence rules the lovesick —
such a grown-up idea.

. . . now the question is
does her innocence turn canny
at the breach of sweet decline

or is it a simple grace
           that saves her
— grandma's *tinkling* laughter
parting the black surround?

well-well my dear —
Love is the disease/the answer —
the less love pities the beast . . .

Dream

p**A**rtner

whe**R**e—

so blac**K** /

so su**N**less

— no l**I**ght.

Gladness —

Hear

This.

fate/a conversation with a friend (sonora)

i've spent a little over 20 years
in the desert — lost in the declensions
of pattern and detail:

no great love or hope of it —
no real success in the world to hold me
in good stead.

yet just now — i find
i'm no longer so reclusive.
i suffer a dram of bitterness/
an occasional fit of spite —

but my *boon* is my freedom:
the great revelation of the disconnect —
just me —

at home with the thrill —
my diminished fear of solitude.

❖ trifle/isn't it romance?

left at the altar the would-be
bride receives a note
from the missing groom —
it begins:

dearest —
27 cans of peaches in heavy syrup . . .

dumbfounded/cast out
from promise — twinned —
in that moment — with errant desire

. . .
she does — in-her-folly — weep.

exeunt/jean renoir in the catskills

blushed/
carnation pinked —
sipping vodka lemonades

— pursuing
damselflies around
cattails — through reeds/
marsh-y-grass into muddy breach —
we

rush —
ankle deep . . .
streaks of clouds —
you/me for appetizers —
singsonging:

chez nous/entre nous —

sifting diamonds. moonrise —
sheet lightning ta-ta-tattooing —
a-wedding

of spheres and lapses —
chez/entre
nous . . .

[the harvest moon departs]

:
my love-y-dear —
sweetest best and last —
adieu?

wooing/one more frog goes a-courtin'

a conquistador
grazes among
the wild grape —

uh-huh —
goes cloud-mad/
pinked & pearl-y.

i
sing you
sit and spin —

miss-mouse-are-you-within?
big-black snake/
kind-sir — lay down

your
sword and pistol —
your big-loud-roar . . .

lilies —
flames will-grow
beneath our feet.

emeralds —
ancient eyes
will-crown our sleep . . .

you'll
come-a-courtin'/leaping
sweetgrass — my bumb-lee-bee

— uh-huh.

your **P***erfect*

*he***A***rt*

R*ises &*

*fall***S** —

*s***I***mple*

F*ool*

— *m***A***de*

*for g***L***ory.*

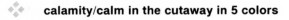

calamity/calm in the cutaway in 5 colors

above —
a swift-scud
of Atomic Orange/
Shell Pink/Gold bits
of sky-tuft —

a Charcoal deckled-
edge
— traverses
the remote-high air.

at zero elevation . . .
sifting through
debris:

an Orange-y Gray
haze sits
heavy

in my palm — occludes
— not-the-stars —

but my hand outstretched —
the far-scribble of mackerel sky.

rakshasi/into the unknown unknown

demon night —
see the naked woman
pretending to be a gorilla
following after a cat chasing
a frenzied squirrel along the fence.
her glee/her zeal is her triumph —
        her justification
for her abandonment of all she knows
for the possibility/the slim chance of slipping
into a world she never/ever —
would've/could've —
guessed . . . [?].

on-reflection/whose words?

we all tell reductive stories of our lives
that are for the most part dependent
on someone/something other being the driver
of our circumstances — though most of us
don't seem to know this. we say
X-Y- or Z made me thus/did to me this . . .
i . . .

is it presumptuous
to even think/say — *i stand by my word(s)?*

well — yes/no/it depends?

persona(e).
i doubt self-drama — doubt the sanctity of ego —
the ownership of all those details that make
a story/that decorate our masks seems

to me up for grabs.
(Go — Kachina Dancers . . .).

& who exactly demanded that tattoo?
so what does this mean — only one
amorphous picture on a platen?
only one overarching idea — mine/not-mine?

i'm no buddhist — but for now
i'm apparently in love — an inamorata
of emptiness.

watershed/water divide

Marianne Moore once lived just around the corner —
some days her distinctive hat
　　　　floats among the plane trees . . .
　　　　　　　　　　　　oak & maple —
the more recent plantings of callery pear.

on sundays — she still sits 3-square
in the capacious heart of the presbyterian church
2 blocks down.

　　　　later Miss Bishop
& famous others visit her for tea. they talk
of water/water creatures — the circus —
Dylan T. slips whiskey into his cup.

at sunset — cats gather at their windows
to watch the air grow electric — the words
— *all-bristling-glister*
　　　　　　　　— spill-over — slide-down-past-the-
Navy-Yard to Wallabout Bay . . .

where *the-glittering-shades* perform a final brief-
　　　　curtsey —
precisely-eddy-&-roll on into the East River.

reprise/let's try that again

the Dredging flight
from fugue —
un-slippered.

thoughts of cherries
& hollering/hollering
birds.

bits
of paper
wet-pasted against concrete.

Cardinal's
chirping brass —
Rosie-o my Rosie-o

—TWACK-BOOM!
a Bear
enters the kitchen?

idyll/prince hal in 9 colors

me
floating among
the water striders . . .

the fleeting-notion-of
some sweet passerine
Chastened Gold —
a-stripe-of

Apricot
&
Azure Mist —
a-dab-of
Beaver
Bole
Cordovan
Drab —
a-wash-of
Buff/Flavescent:

a-shiver in the heat-haze —
my now dead-daddy/the dand-y-lion
— an apparition
sleeping-off a drunk
propped against a tree.

ah —
now that i look more closely —
i see — those striders are boatmen —
diminutive charons

skimming along a-Bitumen-phosphorescence:
how long/how far have i drifted?

❖

kiss Me
kIss me
— Set my
hearT
fLames —
sweEt
moTh
On
firE.

prairie/around the campfire

scatter
me across
the soughing grass —

abloom —
skip-sing-
to-m'-lou my darling.

salvation's
cotton candy —
your sugar dear —

spooling through amber.
heart's a-skipping
fast . . .

tremble & spark
— aglow —
we're a-shimmer —

mystery-cat's
in the cream —
oo oo . . .

❖ valentine/a little a lot not at all in 3 colors

i-wonder —
a tra-lah/a dirge

— a . . . /

boulevard
of bold-Black-cypresses
limned in Persian Rose/

starfish —
tiny gullets
all done up —
agape/agog in Hollywood
Cerise?

balefire/funeral pyre in 3 colors

radial-axis-wheel
i pinwheel-feint —
spit out fireballs

— un-
button teardrops —
Obsidian — i annihilate

all
that is
shape shifting — blown.

in-sorrow
— my plain
distaff's gilded White —

in-thorns
— my rambler
Rose — *ashes ashes?*

dead/yet still our neurons fire back hello

i don't know a lot about death —
not a promising start for a poem. i do know
when my father died his pendulum clock
did stop on the odd minute — twelve/twenty-seven
— and i found meaning and comfort in that ceasing
moment — in that . . . *what?*
                                   the breath
between living and my imagining

of . . . *what?*
and — as the years pass — i do know my sympathy
for who he was accumulates —
i consider his pain as i grow into him year by year
                      . . . i reinvent his promise
— mend all that was broken.

❖ expectant/in 4 colors

triumph over thaw — a sea-glass-haze —
a rufous hawk — the Stil de Grain Yellow
of budding-field-grass

. . . dreaming of Beau Blue —
the hair on my arm startles in the Bronze
light of early mid-day —
a sign of may/june's Copper Rose?

goodbye/going & gone?

the hindu part of me will be cremated on a saturday.
the catholic part will be buried in the midst of incense
          and unreconstructed church latin.
the jewish part will be consoled by the sounds of kaddish.
the animist part of me will be a whirly-whirly —
a dust- or sun-devil skipping from this desert
to that dry prairie or plain until i rise far above this earth
— far/far-and-away beyond ideas of divinity
          and stardust.

but however many disparate ways i find myself allotted —
in my last/possible moment —

                              i promise to honor us all
— what was mine i give to you and you.

CPSIA information can be obtained at www.ICGtesting.com
Printed in the USA
LVOW11s1655200214

374547LV00006B/943/P